CAN I HAVE
A COOKIE?

By BIL KEANE

FAWCETT GOLD MEDAL • NEW YORK

CAN I HAVE A COOKIE?

Published by Fawcett Gold Medal Books, CBS Educational and Professional Publishing, a division of CBS Inc., by arrangement with The Register & Tribune Syndicate, Inc.

ISBN: 0-449-14155-1

Printed in the United States of America

31 30 29 28 27 26 25 24 23 22 21

"Billy says the doctor will use hedge shears like Daddy's to take my tonsils out."

"It's all right for you to take your blanket to the
hospital with you, but let's carry
it in this paper bag."

"Don't worry, Jeffy, while you're in the hospital
we'll be prayin' for you all the time. Can
I play with your monster maker?"

"NOW I 'member being here before—that time
when I got borned!"

"You're not ready to go home yet, Love--that was just the blood test."

"Why do I have to wear a baby's bracelet and sleep in a CRIB? Don't they know I'm almost FIVE?"

"I can't sleep in here very good 'cause I can't hear Daddy watchin' TV or Mommy doing the dishes or Barfy barking or P.J crying..."

"I won't get hurt, Mommy, they fastened my
seat belts."

"I think they forgot to take out my tonsils 'cause my throat is very sore."

"That Jeffy's LUCKY! He's lyin' around getting
all the popsicles he wants and sodas
and watching TV..."

"We're going home now, Jeffy—say good-bye
to the nurses and w.."

"They only gave Jeffy his tonsils to bring home
from the hospital—they didn't give him a baby."

"Mommy! Can you button this for me?"

"I think somebody's ready for breakfast."

"Thel, how many children's aspirin do I take to make two adult ones?"

"THIS IS THE DAWNING OF THE AGE
OF ASPARAGUS..."

"Well, hello there, little man! What a cute little feller! How'd you like to come home with ME?"

"Daddy, turn your eyes on."

"I guess I didn't grow as much as Grandma thought I did."

"You fell out of bed? Well, how did you manage to roll 'way down here?"

"PJ must be really growing! He used to be able
to walk under that table without
bumping his head!"

"I wanna go faster, Mommy! RUN!"

"Hi, Grandma! Mommy hopes to heaven you
didn't bring us more candy, but we
hope to heaven you did!"

"I have to cut out pictures of a 'P' sound. Does
PASKETTI begin with a 'B' or a 'P'?"

"If you find any hairs in the food, Grandma,
don't worry about it. They're just
Barfy's or Sam's."

"How can Aunt Kay be my AUNT and my GODMOTHER, too?"

"You'll recognize our house -- it's the one with
bare spots on the lawn, toys in the driveway
and fingerprints around the front door."

"Guess what we all decided to do for dinner
tonight, Daddy! Can we go with you
to pick up Grandma?"

"Here's your cupcake, Daddy. I only dropped
it once, but I licked it off."

"Mommy says we have to come in the house
RIGHT NOW!"

"Jeffy touched my new shoes without washing his hands first."

"Can everybody stay for lunch, Mommy?"

"We're playing sailor! Billy's captain, Dolly's cook and I'm first bait!"

"Mommy! Billy used a four-legged word!"

"I winned! I reached him first!"

"What did we used to watch before
football season?"

"Don't be too rough with Dolly! Remember—
she's just a little GIRL!"

"Mommy won't let us buy that kind 'cause there's something on the box to send away for."

"Can we come home with you and see all your cows?"

"See? Everytime I say I had it first an' YOU say
YOU had it first, Mommy's the one that gets it."

"Shake!"

"Can we go around without PJ? He lifts his mask up and everybody knows who we are."

"Under...around...over...and THROUGH!"

"The only thing I don't like about visiting
Grandma, is her 'partment has too
many no-no's in it."

"Grandma, are you going to eat all of these
lollipops in your drawer?"

"Don't put it in a glass, Grandma! I can drink it out of the bottle!"

"But we don't need money. You could just write another CHECK!"

"Wanna make a wish, Daddy?"

"Can PJ take an early nap today?"

"Mommy said your eyes are bigger than your tummy and that means your tummy is THIS BIG."

"This is the Saturday I go over to Steve O'Connor's to work on our project. Who's gonna drive me?"

"Look, Mommy! This one banana's smiling and this other one's sad."

"I've got a great big cut on my leg. As soon as
I find it I'll show it to you!"

"I wrote a letter to Grandma. What did I say?"

"Why did you have to pay the lady to get our coats back?"

"I stirred the paint for you, but I didn't mean to."

"Guess who won!"

"Don't act tired or we'll all have to go home!"

"Did you see a fly go this way?"

"Which one of you children has my good scissors?"

"We don't have to pay you as much for sitting as we pay Mrs. Young."

"Daddy, will you tell PJ to stay inside the lines if he doesn't want to get hit?"

"Mommy! PJ flushed away all the toothbrushes!"

"First there was God. Next came George
Washington, and then Daddy."

"MY turn! MY turn! Mommy said the new cup
'spencer is for EVERYBODY!"

"Daddy's home, Mommy! Aren't you going to
run out and meet him?"

"CAN-N-N-DY!"

"Yours is lovely, too, PJ! It says 'To Mommy—
Be My Valentine...'"

"We didn't hear you those first two times
you called."

"Mommy? Did you find a note in my pocket
about a 'pointment you have with my
teacher at 3 o'clock?"

"Aren't we proud of PJ? He can say his alphabet
up to C, 'cept sometimes he forgets B."

"My regular teacher was absent today and the
art teacher took her place."

"Mommy, do I like this?"

"I can button it for you, Mommy!"   "Thank you, dear."

"'HOUSE' means it's empty. When people move in, it's a 'HOME'."

"I don't SEE any vitamins in here."

"Want me to taste one of those cupcakes for you
to see if they turned out all right?"

"Wanna see my report card, Grandma? Here's
your handbag."

"It was some man, or a lady or somebody...
anyway, they want Daddy to call 'em back."

"Did the dentist let you pick a prize out of the
treasure box for being good?"

"We rinsed off the ice cubes in hot water and now we can't find them!"

"When I turned my report card in, Miss Johnson
wanted to know why you wrote 'X-X-X'
with crayon under your name."

"Hey, Billy! What are you gonna turn into when you grow up?"

"Can we take my bug to the veginarian? I think
he broke his leg."

"Mommy isn't playing on them. She's looking
for my little brother."

"There were TWELVE doughnuts here when we went to bed -- now there are only TEN!"

"We cleaned out under the seats."

"Mommy, was this REALLY s'posed to be my
lunch or did I pick up the wrong bag
when I was leavin' this morning?"

"Outta the way, PJ! You're too little to play
with us guys--you'll get HURT! Go HOME!"

"Don't cry--Mommy will give you hers."

"Wowee! School was tough today! We tried to learn the first two lines of 'Here Comes Peter Cottontail!'."

"I'm s'posed to bring a bunny rabbit costume to
wear in the play today. Lucky I
remembered, isn't it Mommy?"

"Could we put up an EASTER TREE so the bunny
can put presents under it?"

"Coach says I'm to practice throwing to you for
at least 15 minutes every night."

"We keep saying 'Rain, rain, go away, come again another day,' but it doesn't work."

"We can't find the spot where we buried our treasure. It's a coffee can with a penny in it."

"Did Jeffy say how sorry he is for putting that
ice cube down my dress today?"

"Is this one a weed?"

"It's a good thing this didn't happen driving TO
the train or Daddy might've been late for work!"

"PJ drank the dribbles of coffee out of your cup!
Will that stump his growth?"

"Hey, Mister! Isn't my mommy PRETTY in her
new bathin' suit?"

"Campers Anonymous? Look—we have an uncontrollable urge to go camping again. Can you send someone over to talk us out of it?"

"Make sure the turtle has food and water,
Grandma and put fresh leaves in for the
bugs. The frog's water will need
changin', and the snake eats..."

"Mommy, can we go in the house and watch TV
while Daddy is trying to back out
of the driveway?"

"BYE, HOUSE! We'll send you a postcard!"

"Why do the steep hills in the road ahead always
FLATTEN OUT when we start to climb 'em?"

"BILLY!"..."Here."..."DOLLY!"..."Here."
..."JEFFY!"..."Here."..."PJ!"..."Here."
..."BARFY!"..."SAM?"...

"Hooray! We're here! Let's make a fire,
Daddy, and put up the tent!"

"It says: 'Remember—only YOU can prevent forest fires'."

"Will you put some of this sunburn lotion on me, Mommy?"

"Wake up, everybody! Dinner's finally ready."

"I can't get to sleep with all those stars shining in my eyes."

"But two pounds of hamburger is always PLENTY
for us at home."

"Is it almost moming?"
"No, it's ten past nine."

"Aren't you glad you're not WORKIN' this week, Daddy?"

"Shh! Nobody move...Don't make a sound..."

"Jeffy didn't wash his hands!"

"But I'm afraid to walk over there alone. You
come with me."

"...and my mommy can't wait to get home into a bathtub, and Daddy hopes he never sees another sleepin' bag, and my little brother has ivy poison all over--even on his bottom, and we...
I think I hear Mommy calling me."

"Know what, Mister? We've been CAMPING!"

"Can we sleep outside in the back yard tonight?"

"I can't sleep 'cause the bed's too soft and I can't hear the frogs and crickets and all that stuff."